WITHDRAWN

The Library of
NATIVE AMERICANS

The Oneida
of Wisconsin

Gillian Houghton

The Rosen Publishing Group's
PowerKids Press™
New York

The author wishes to acknowledge the encouragement and expertise of
Dr. Carol Cornelius of the Oneida Cultural Heritage Department.

Published in 2003 by The Rosen Publishing Group, Inc.
29 East 21st Street, New York, NY 10010

Photo and Illustration Credits: Cover and pp. 13, 15, 16, 30, 50 , 55 courtesy Oneida Nation Museum; p. 4 Erica Clendening; p. 7 Logan Museum of Anthropology at Beloit College, Beloit, WI (LMA–6918); p. 8 courtesy of the New York State Museum, Albany, New York; pp. 18, 27, 45 © Bettmann/CORBIS; pp. 21, 42, 46 © CORBIS; p. 24 © Francis G. Mayer/CORBIS; p. 29 Library of Congress, Manuscript Division; pp. 35, 39, 41, 48 Milwaukee Public Museum; p. 36 Smithsonian American Art Museum, Washington, DC/Art Resource, NY; p. 52 © Lisa A. Fifield.

Book Design: Erica Clendening

Houghton, Gillian.
    The Oneida of Wisconsin / Gillian Houghton.
        p. cm. — (The library of Native Americans)
    ISBN 0-8239-6432-9
    Includes bibliographical references and index.
    1. Oneida Indians—History—Juvenile literature 2. Oneida Indians—Social life and customs—Juvenile literature. [1. Oneida Indians. 2. Indians of North America—New York (State).] I. Title. II. Series.
    E99.O45 H84 2002
    974.7004'9755—dc21

                                             2002002320

Manufactured in the United States of America

Contents

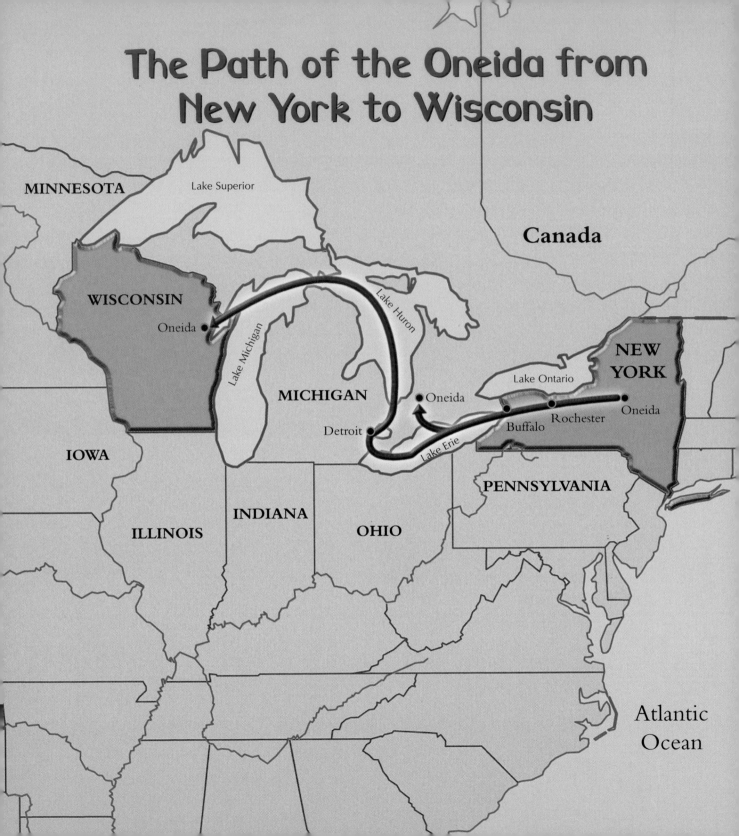

The Path of the Oneida from New York to Wisconsin

One

Introducing the Oneida People

The Oneida are an ancient people whose long journey led them to their current home in Wisconsin. In the Oneida language, they are called *Onayoteaka*, which means "People of the Standing Stone." They trace their ancestors and their traditional culture to the rolling hills and white pine forests of what is known today as central New York. In New York, they joined with four other Native American nations to form a powerful alliance. The Thanksgiving Address, which is recited before all meetings and ceremonies, lists the elements of the natural world for which they are thankful: Mother Earth, the grasses and small plants that provide food and medicine, strawberries, trees, animals, water and water animals, the Three Sisters (corn, beans, and squash), birds, winds, Grandfathers the thunderers, Grandmother moon, the stars, Elder Brother the sun, the four messengers, and the Creator. The arrival of Europeans—first explorers and traders, then missionaries, then frontier settlers—changed the Oneida nation forever.

When Europeans arrived in North America, they introduced an understanding of the world that was different from that of the Oneida. They believed in a different god, spoke a different language, and organized their societies with different rules and principles. For

This map illustrates where the Oneidas lived. Originally part of the Iroquois Confederacy in New York, they traveled west, settling in present-day Wisconsin. A group of Oneidas also settled in Canada.

many years the Oneida were divided over how to respond to the Europeans. Some embraced the European way of life, while others rejected it. The Europeans claimed authority over the lands that the Oneida had held for generations. In order to survive, some Oneidas chose to move west to a new home on a reservation in the Wisconsin frontier. In moving from their ancient homeland, the Oneida combined their traditional beliefs and customs with new ways of life. Soon, reservation life in Wisconsin was troubled by new U.S. laws and approaching settlements and business interests. The Oneida once again faced the question of how to maintain their beliefs and secure their land. They lost much of their land, which was the fabric of their communities. The people of the reservation faced unemployment and homelessness.

In the last fifty years, the Oneida of Wisconsin have revived their traditional culture and continue to be a sovereign nation, while other Oneida continue to live in New York and Canada. The nation is a strong, independent community that is home to Native Americans and non-Native Americans. Today, tribal elders work to preserve a culture that was almost lost and to share it with the next generation of Oneida.

Generations of Oneida craftspeople were experts in the traditional art of basketry. This black ash basket was made for use in daily life, and many baskets were traded with non-Native Americans.

Two

Oneida Government and Cultural Traditions

Some archaeological records suggest that the Oneida may have lived on the land that is now called New York when the first humans roamed North America. Other evidence tells us these nations originally lived in the southeast and migrated north along the east coast of North America sometime before the earliest known oral or written records.

The Oneida were one of the five nations that founded the Iroquois Confederacy, a group of northeastern Native American nations that joined together to protect one another. Some experts say that they united in the 1500s, while others believe that it occurred much earlier, in ancient times. The other original member nations were the Mohawk, Onondaga, Cayuga, and Seneca. In the 1700s, a sixth nation, the Tuscarora Nation, joined the confederacy, and the group became known as the Six Nations. The confederacy created a council of chiefs, incorporating a certain number of chiefs from each nation. The council worked to protect the Six Nations from any outside threat and maintain peace between the nations.

When the Iroquois Confederacy was created, the Oneidas lived on a wide strip of land in central New York State that stretched from the St. Lawrence River in the north to the modern-day Pennsylvania

Like other members of the Iroquois Confederacy, the Oneidas' traditional type of home is the longhouse. This replica shows how it was built. Wooden poles were tied together to create the framework, which was then covered with large sheets of elm bark.

border in the south. The land included most of Oneida Lake and the Oneida Portage Way, which was valuable because it connected Wood Creek and the Mohawk River, linking southeast New York with the Great Lakes of the midwest and Canada. It was a fertile land, dotted with thick white pine forests, freshwater lakes, and rolling hills. Wild game was plentiful, and the ground was good for farming.

Life in the Longhouse

The Oneida of New York lived in villages made up of several structures called longhouses, which were surrounded by a strong fence called a palisade. The longhouse dated to the creation of the Iroquois Confederacy, when, according to legend, the Peacemaker brought order and unity to the Native American nations. The longhouse was symbolic of the close family ties of the Iroquois, with all people of the same clan living together under one roof. Each longhouse was about one hundred feet (30 m) long and twenty-five feet (8 m) wide. Two rows of thick poles were set in the ground about twenty feet apart. The tops of the poles were lashed together, forming a curved roof that was supported by a single row of upright posts running down the center of the house. At either end, poles were set in the ground to make vertical walls. The entire frame was covered with sheets of bark, creating a watertight wall with doors at both ends and holes in the roof for smoke to escape. During the winter, the longhouse walls were insulated.

The inside of each longhouse was divided into several twenty-foot-long (6 m) areas along the center aisle of the house. Each area housed a different nuclear family, all of whom were related to a single matriarch, or female elder. When a man married a woman, he went to live with her family, and their children were considered members of their mother's clan, or group. The three clans that were central to Oneida identity and politics were Wolf, Bear, and Turtle. Each clan's longhouse had their animal symbol over their door. Families built sleeping platforms and places to store food and supplies in their area. They slept on reed mats under warm animal skins. Hearths for cooking and keeping warm were made in the center aisle and shared by the families on either side.

The meeting of the Grand Council is an Iroquois tradition that still occurs to this day. The Grand Council is made up of fifty chiefs. In the beginning, there were nine Mohawk, nine Oneida, fourteen Onondaga, ten Cayuga, and eight Seneca chiefs on the Grand Council. The chiefs meet at least once each year. Issues are raised and debated by the clans in each nation. The chiefs discuss each issue with their nation's people and bring their decision to the Grand Council meeting. Each nation has one vote, which is recorded by the Onondaga Fire Keepers.

Daily Life

The Oneida got their food by hunting and farming. The men hunted white tail deer, rabbit, bear, and wild turkeys. The meat was eaten and the hide and bones were used to make clothing, shoes, and many domestic tools. The men also caught salmon and other fish in Oneida Lake and in the Mohawk, Oswego, and Oneida Rivers. The women were responsible for planting and harvesting crops. Their method of cleaning the land was called swidden, or slash-and-burn. An area of land would be burned to clear the trees and bushes, allowing new crops to be planted in their place. Over time, new lands would be cultivated while the already used areas were left unplanted, allowing the soil to replenish its supply of minerals. This method conserved the land and made it rich and fertile for future generations. Corn, beans, and squash, known as the Three Sisters of Oneida farming, were planted in hills and harvested each year. They were important foods in the Oneida diet and important cultural symbols.

The Oneida also made and decorated many types of crafts. Children played with dolls made out of dried corn husks. The Oneida also made distinctive pottery that was decorated with images of squash and beans.

Women gathered wild berries, nuts, and fruits for food and medicine. They dried fish, fruits, and vegetables and traded them with

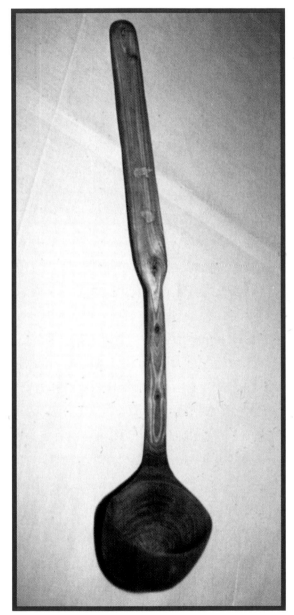

other Native American communities. By preserving their natural resources, they created an economy that respected the delicate relationship between humans and nature.

The early Native Americans of New York celebrated the festivals of the farming calendar, passed down stories about their people from one generation to the next, and played *ga-lahs*, or lacrosse, in Oneida. *Ga-lahs* was good exercise and had sacred and medicinal significance within the Iroquois community.

This wooden spoon is a modern-day replica of a utensil traditionally made by the Oneida.

Upholder-of-the-Skies

For many generations, the Oneida have maintained a rich oral tradition. An oral tradition consists of the stories that people tell one another from generation to generation. The Oneida creation story tells how the Sky-woman fell out of the sky world and landed on the back of the turtle. The Oneida tell the story to explain how the world was created and to understand good and evil. The Oneida have told this story for centuries, and although most of it has remained the same, there have been some variations.

According to the Oneida creation story, the world we now know was once covered by a vast body of water. Turtles, fish, and other animals swam in the waters, and sea birds flew overhead. Humans lived in another world high in the sky. In this sky world, there was no sickness or death. The people did not feel jealousy or anger. However, one day a man ordered that a tree be uprooted. When his pregnant wife tried to look through the hole in the ground left by the uprooted tree, she fell in. As she fell through the deep hole, she grasped a strawberry plant in one hand and a tobacco plant in the other. She continued to fall through the dark sky. The animals in the water below saw her approaching and met together in a council to decide what to do. After some discussion, they agreed to build a world for her.

Loons caught the falling woman and placed her safely on a turtle's back. The animals decided that the world should be built on the back of the turtle, the strongest of the animals of the water. The muskrat swam to the depths of the water to gather mud to build solid ground on the turtle's back, but the muskrat drowned. When his body was found, the animals discovered a small piece of mud clutched in his paw. The mud was placed on the turtle's back. From this bit of earth, the whole world grew. By the next morning, the ground had spread out under her feet, forming the earth, with streams and rivers leading to an expanse of ocean. Sky-woman soon gave birth to a daughter. The daughter quickly grew to be an adult, and several animals disguised as men came to ask for her hand in marriage.

An Oneida craftsperson decorated this handbag with beaded designs. Creating pictures or patterns with beads is a slow and precise process, which the Oneidas believe was given to them by Creator to teach patience and humility.

15

The west wind came to the young woman one night as she slept and lay two crossed arrows on her stomach. One arrow had a point made of flint, and the other arrow had a point made of soft wood. In time, the young woman gave birth to twin sons. The impatient elder son, often called Flint, burst through his mother's left armpit, killing her as she gave birth to him and his brother, who is often known as Upholder-of-the-Skies. The twins grew and became young men. Flint was an expert hunter and his grandmother's favorite, but he also created evil. Upholder-of-the-Skies, however, created all of the blessings on Earth.

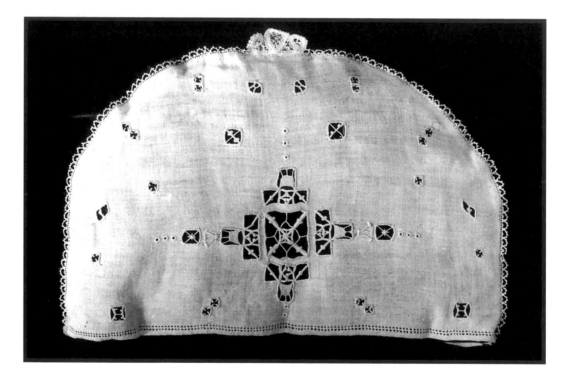

This lace doily was made by Josephine Webster, Oneida tribal member.

There was competition between the two young twins as they arranged the world. Upholder-of-the-Skies made all of the rivers of the world flow in both directions, so that people could travel easily from one place to the next. Flint changed the course of the rivers, creating rapids and dangerous passes. Upholder-of-the-Skies responded by creating portages, or sturdy banks of land, so humans could avoid the dangerous rapids. Upholder-of-the-Skies gave life to game animals, so that humans could always have creatures to hunt, but Flint locked the game away and created dangerous animals like wolves, snakes, and wildcats. The good twin responded by releasing the game animals into the wild and making sure that the dangerous animals would rarely harm humans.

Upholder-of-the-Skies is responsible for all that is good on Earth. His gift to the Oneida was the Three Sisters, which represent the three main crops planted by the Oneida: corn, beans, and squash. His name is sometimes translated as the Great Spirit or the Good Spirit. In later versions, he is also responsible for teaching humans to gather as a family and perform the prayers and dances of Thanksgiving that unite the Oneida people as a spiritual community. The Oneida believe that every thing has a spirit, including wind, fire, trees, and lakes. The Oneida give thanks to the spirits in seasonal festivals of Thanksgiving. The Maple Festival, Planting Festival, Strawberry Festival, Green Corn Festival, Harvest Festival, and New Year celebration mark important events in nature's yearly cycle.

Three

Encounters with the Europeans

Many years before the Dutch arrived in New York in 1609, the Oneida and other Iroquois Native Americans had a trade network with other Native American nations and European visitors. However, with the establishment of a small Dutch trade empire in the northeast, the economy changed from small-scale hunting to an international fur trade market. Trapping wild animals and trading their furs became one of the most important aspects of Oneida life. The Europeans traded knives, brass kettles, scissors, and cloth for the Native Americans' fox, mink, beaver, and bear fur.

By the 1630s, the demand for fur overwhelmed the natural supply, and the populations of wild game dwindled. Competition became fierce, and disagreements within and between nations began to form. The Oneidas and other Six Nation tribes raided Native American villages in Canada and as far south as Virginia, stealing trade goods and killing Native Americans. Eventually, the governor of Canada responded. In 1696, he attacked the Oneida and Onondaga villages, burning them to the ground.

The Europeans also brought contagious diseases, such as smallpox and measles, to North America. The Europeans were immune

This painting by Alonzo Chappel shows George Washington's army suffering through a cold winter during the American Revolution. The Oneida brought several hundred bags of corn to feed the starving army.

to these diseases, but the Oneidas and other Native Americans were not. Many historians believe that these illnesses killed nearly half of the Oneida population. These deaths had a devastating effect on the Oneida. The men and women who died of European diseases were the mothers, fathers, elders, chiefs, warriors, planters, and children of the Oneida nation. Communities were left without their leaders, storytellers, and providers.

Iroquois Confederacy During the American Revolution

The structure of the Oneida community was threatened, as was the Iroquois Confederacy. The American Revolution (1775–1783) brought these tensions between and within the Six Nations to the fore. The Mohawk, Seneca, Onondaga, and Cayuga nations were loyalists, faithful to the crown of England. The Oneidas and Tuscaroras fought on behalf of the American revolutionaries, who called themselves patriots. In many Iroquois villages, there were disagreements between the warriors and the chiefs over the nations' involvement in the war. Many tried to stay neutral. The Oneidas fought bravely at several important battles during the Revolution. Many served as scouts and spies, but their involvement in the war divided the Oneida nation internally and distanced them from other Iroquois nations.

In many cases, the Oneida warriors fought against their own Iroquois confederates on the battlefield and, led by American generals, raided Iroquois villages. In response, Seneca, Onondaga, Cayuga, and Mohawk warriors attacked Oneida villages, burning their homes to the ground. As more Oneidas joined the efforts of the American revolutionaries and took up arms against the British and their fellow Iroquois, families and villages began to suffer. The history of the Oneida had entered a new era, which would be one of bloodshed, starvation, and displacement.

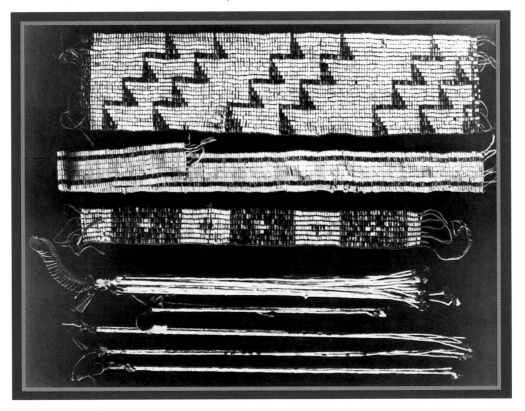

The Iroquois made beaded belts from wampum to record special events. At the end of the American Revolution, the Oneida made a wampum belt to signify the reunification of Iroquois Confederacy.

The Great Awakening

In the midst of this tension and change, a young Presbyterian missionary settled on the Oneida lands sixteen miles from Fort Stanwix, New York. His name was Samuel Kirkland, and he would significantly change the face of the Oneida community. Kirkland's spirituality was the product of a popular American Christian religious movement of the early 1700s called the Great Awakening. The Great Awakening focused on an individual's search for religious truth. This practice was unlike the Oneida's communal religion, which included group prayer and celebration. Kirkland first brought his Christian message to the Oneida in August 1766. He won converts among the Oneida, who mixed Kirkland's Christian message with their own traditional beliefs.

Kirkland's message focused on education and moral reform. Many Oneidas agreed that real changes would have to be made if the nation was going to survive in the newly-formed United States. Large-scale farming and abstinence from alcohol were the focus of Kirkland's plan for a new Oneida nation. In 1794, he established the Hamilton-Oneida Academy, a school for the moral and practical education of the Oneidas. The school taught reading, writing, and methods of agriculture. Classes were taught in English. The real intention of the school was to convert and assimilate Oneidas. It was one of many "civilization programs" created to control or remove the Native Americans as whites settled closer to their tribal lands.

Some Oneidas embraced Kirkland's message. His teachings started to divide the Oneida nation between those who chose to follow Christianity, and those who maintained the traditional ways. As white settlements extended farther north and west, the two groups would debate one issue more than any other: How could the Oneida best protect their land and their way of life?

Four

The New York State Treaties

In 1784, when the American Revolution had come to an end, the new government of the United States met with the Six Nations at Fort Stanwix. The Continental Congress, wishing to drive the four Iroquois nations that had fought for the British out of New York, imposed strict rules and limited territorial boundaries on the Mohawk, Seneca, Onondaga, and Cayuga people. Congress considered the Oneidas their allies. In the Treaty of 1784, Congress promised the Oneida nation never to threaten their lands.

In 1790, Congress passed the Trade and Non-Intercourse Act, which made it illegal for individuals or state governments to negotiate treaties with Native American nations without the approval of a U.S. commission appointed by the president. This law was meant to protect the Native Americans, but many people, such as New York governor George Clinton, simply ignored it. Despite the government's promises, by the beginning of the nineteenth century the Oneida had lost all but a few hundred acres of their vast six-million-acre New York territory.

In 1792, Congress approved the sum of $1,500 to be paid yearly to the Six Nations in exchange for their peace and friendship. In 1794, Congress repeated this promise and added $3,000, bringing

As governor of New York, George Clinton persuaded the Oneida to sell parts of their land to the state government. Clinton then sold the land to companies who forced the Oneida from their homes.

the total to $4,500. Today, the U.S. government continues to pay this amount to the Six Nations. The Oneida's yearly portion is $1,800. These terms were recorded in the Treaty of Canandaigua. This treaty is known as the Calico Treaty, for the fabric offered in payment to the Native Americans. It is also called the Pickering Treaty, for Indian Commissioner and Secretary of War Timothy Pickering.

Throughout the American Revolution, General Philip Schuyler was considered a friend and a protector of the Oneida. He had recruited Oneida warriors and led them into battle, praising their bravery and commitment. He often spoke of his wish to see the Oneida free and at peace. He was also a vocal supporter of repaying the Oneidas for their efforts in the war. However, Philip Schuyler was also a businessman who was interested in making a profit. As the surveyor general of New York, and later as a United States senator, Schuyler recognized the vast potential of New York's natural resources. He was eager to control New York's primary transportation routes, including rivers, lakes, and roads, which would give him control over all of the commerce in the state. Oneida Country was the natural crossroads of central New York.

Using the influence of his powerful family, Schuyler was appointed as one of four New York Indian Commissioners and became responsible for negotiating treaties with the Six Nations. In this position, Schuyler systematically broke the law and tricked the Oneida into giving up ownership of millions of acres of land. Schuyler put on the appearance of friendship by publicly speaking in defense of the

Oneida. He gave money to the missionary efforts of Samuel Kirkland, who named the Hamilton-Oneida Academy after Schuyler's son-in-law, Alexander Hamilton. In return, Kirkland voiced his support for the sale of Oneida land to the government and independent land speculators, such as Schuyler. Kirkland, who had been a genuine friend to the Oneida during the war, now led them to the treaty table and watched them sign away their ancestral homelands.

Schuyler also exerted his influence on Governor Clinton. Throughout the late eighteenth century, Clinton made aggressive and sometimes illegal efforts to acquire Oneida land. The first of these swindles was a 1785

When he was a general in the American Revolution, Philip Schuyler fought alongside Oneida soldiers and helped reward them for their bravery. However, when he became the surveyor general of New York, he tried to control the state's transportation routes by tricking the Oneida into giving away their land.

treaty in which the state of New York purchased 300,000 acres of land in the southern Oneida territory for a fraction of its value. The Oneidas were eager to maintain peace with the new state government and asked Clinton to promise that he would never try to buy any more Oneida land. Only three years later, in 1788, Clinton returned to the Oneidas and encouraged them to sell or lease five-and-a-half million acres, nearly all of their land, to the state of New York. The governor claimed that this would protect the Oneida from the encroaching white settlements. However, his real motive was to obtain the land for himself. He claimed the right to buy the land before anyone else and then to sell it to various land companies and businessmen. After several days of debate, the Oneidas agreed to the governor's proposal, dividing their lands into three sections and placing two-thirds of it in the care of the state.

The Oneidas believed that the treaty would maintain peace and secure their lands from outside interests, but the treaty proved to be devastating in the loss of the Oneida's land base. Clinton continued to trick and pressure the Oneidas. The state government illegally gave small groups of Oneidas the power to enter treaties on behalf of the entire Oneida nation, then proceeded to buy hundreds of thousands of acres of land without the approval of Congress. Although Secretary of War Pickering tried to stop Clinton, he eventually gave up, refusing to spend federal money to battle the inevitable loss of Native American lands.

This July 11, 1777 letter was a report to Philip Schuyler by Oneida Indians sent into Canada. During their interactions with New York officials, the Oneidas lost millions of acres of land.

Five

Eleazer Williams Leads the Oneida to Wisconsin

At the beginning of the nineteenth century, the Oneidas, now numbering about 1,200, lived on a small strip of land around Oneida Lake. The community was divided between those who had converted to Christianity, forming a group that called itself the Christian Party, and those who had kept their traditional beliefs, whom the Christians called the Pagan Party. The two groups lived apart from each other.

The people faced near starvation each winter. Wild game became scarce as white settlements moved in on the traditional Oneida hunting grounds. The Native American nation was plagued by alcohol abuse. Alcohol had been introduced by Europeans through trade and was consumed while making treaties. By losing their land, the Oneida had lost the means of supporting their economy and traditional way of life. The ancient tribal structure continued to break down, and the Oneida became divided over issues concerning their relationship with the state and U.S. governments.

In addition, the Oneida now experienced pressure to give up their few remaining acres of New York land to make way for the surge of white settlements in New York. The Ogden Land Company had been given the right to settle the Six Nations' land when the government acquired the land. As white settlers flooded into New

This is a 1917 photo of Oneida lace makers. From left to right are: Josephine Webster, Tillie Baird, Angeline Hill, and Mrs. Levinia John. Oneida women became famous for their lace making. A large portion of their yearly income came from the sale of lace.

York, the company, led by Congressman David A. Ogden, became more eager to acquire Oneida land and see the complete removal of all Native Americans to territories farther west. Many people justified the relocation of the Six Nations by arguing that the Native Americans would be more likely to assimilate into white society if they could be free of the pressures and vices brought about by the white settlements. Others argued that this policy clearly broke the promises made to the Native American in treaties made in 1784, 1789, and 1794.

Eleazer Williams's personal history has always been a mystery. Little is known of his childhood before his enrollment in a white New England school. He often claimed that he was the lost dauphin, or prince, of France. His claim has since been proven false by DNA testing of the remains of the "real" prince, a boy who died in prison in 1795 at the age of ten.

In 1816, a St. Regis Native American named Eleazer Williams moved to the Oneida reservation. An Episcopalian minister who spoke Mohawk and English, Williams quickly earned followers among the Christians and formed a group that called itself the First Christian Party. The following year, the chiefs of the Pagan Party also converted, forming the Second Christian Party. Williams served as an interpreter and representative in the Oneidas' dealings with missionaries and Indian agents, earning him the respect and trust of many in the Oneida nation in New York. Williams seems to have been genuinely interested in creating and leading an Iroquois empire in the west. However, like Samuel Kirkland, Williams lost the respect of his followers as the interests of white investors overwhelmed his religious enthusiasm.

Williams joined forces with the Ogden Land Company and the War Department to bring about the removal of the Oneidas from their New York homeland. Letters written by Williams to Ogden and other prominent New Yorkers illustrate that Ogden and the federal government financed Williams' efforts to relocate the Oneidas in the west and paid him an additional sum for his work. Secretary of War John Calhoun covered Williams's expenses when the minister traveled to Wisconsin to negotiate with the Menominee and Winnebago for the sale of a small tract land near Green Bay, Wisconsin.

During Williams's travels west, the majority of Oneidas, particularly members of the Second Christian Party, grew distrustful of his reasons for supporting relocation. Many Oneidas petitioned the Episcopal bishop of New York and the federal government to have Williams removed from the reservation. Some Oneidas traveled to Washington to complain directly to Calhoun.

Still, many Oneidas, mostly members of the First Christian Party, supported Williams and were ready to move to Wisconsin. Williams returned to Wisconsin in 1821. He met with the Menominee nation and negotiated a treaty in which he bought the right to inhabit the lands that the Menominee and Winnebago shared. The treaty gave the Oneidas the right to share eight million acres, but the document would be highly contested by the Menominees for many years to come. Despite the disagreements between the Menominee and Oneida, by 1825, 150 Oneidas had taken the long and treacherous journey to the new reservation, settling with Williams and his new wife at Little Kakalin on the Fox River. In 1830, members of the Second Christian Party, which became known as the Orchard Party, moved to Wisconsin. The Pagan Party, however, remained in New York. Between 1832 and 1838, the new, permanent settlement at Duck Creek became home to 654 Oneidas, half of the total Oneida population.

In 1831, the Stambaugh Treaty gave 500,000 acres of Menominee land for New York Native Americans to resettle. This treaty was designed to settle the dispute between the Menominees and Oneida. The treaty of February 3, 1838 defined the boundaries of Oneida lands in Wisconsin by following a subsistence formula of 100 acres for every Oneida then living in Wisconsin. The Wisconsin Oneidas would communally share about 65,400 acres of land. The land that remained, which added up to about 440,000 acres, was handed over or sold for mere pennies per acre to the U.S. government.

This is a 1929 photo of Oneida woman Laura Smith.

Six

Life at Duck Creek

At the beginning of the nineteenth century, central Wisconsin mirrored the New York that the Oneidas had known before the arrival of Dutch fur traders. The rolling hills were covered with thick forests of white pine. The Oneidas hunted game, fished in the Fox River, picked plants for medicines, and harvested berries and nuts for food. They also cleared the land and planted corn, beans, and squash, later adding wheat, oats, and hay. However, the traditional Oneida way of life had changed in several important ways. Farming, which was once the responsibility of women, was now the occupation of men, as it was in white settlements. The traditional Iroquois longhouses were replaced by plastered log cabins and, in many instances, painted, wood frame houses. Many log cabins had outdoor cooking sheds, which replaced the longhouse's central hearth. The women looked after the home, which was now often limited to members of a single nuclear family. This smaller family unit became the center of the Oneida community. Mothers chose wives for sons as young as fourteen years old, and divorce and infidelity were very rare. Family bonds, particularly between brothers and sisters and between grandparents and grandchildren, were very strong.

The Oneida brought many of their traditional practices and beliefs to Wisconsin. Respect for one's elders remained central to

This portrait of Chief Daniel Bread was painted in 1831. As an Oneida chief, Bread fought to give his nation control of the natural resources on its land.

During the American Civil War (1861–1865), many Oneida fought for the Union army. Of the 1,100 Oneidas living on the reservation at the time, historians believe that between 111 and 142 enlisted in the army. Of these soldiers, between forty-six and sixty-five were lost in the war. At that time, Native Americans were not considered U.S. citizens under law, but they could serve as substitutes for those citizens who wished to avoid service. The Native American soldiers were paid for their service. While many Oneida volunteered because they felt it was their patriotic duty, many were tempted by the $300, clothing, regular meals, and monthly pay offered by army recruiters. Joining the army seemed to be a good way for a poor, young farmer to make some money. However, the human losses suffered by the Oneida community during the war were great and further undermined the nation's way of life.

the community and its political organization. Many religious and social traditions based on the planting calendar continued, but were held in secret because Christian priests did not approve of the traditional ceremonies. The community came together to build churches and create mutual aid societies. Traditional medical societies thrived, and the maintenance of the delicate balance between humans and nature remained central to the Oneidas' understanding of the world. Many medical ceremonies, such as the false-face ceremony for curing illnesses, secretly continued.

The presence of these traditional beliefs enabled the Oneida community to balance their traditional values with those they adopted from white society. With the change from living in the longhouse to log cabins came a significant loss of community identity. Clans were no longer the main social and political forces in Oneida villages. Rituals, including marriages and funerals, now centered around the church instead of the clan. Parts of the oral tradition, including the

These two Oneida women are weaving splint baskets. This photo was taken in 1939.

Sky-woman creation story, were incorporated into the Christian belief system, but much of the original meaning was lost. Federal boarding schools punished students who spoke Oneida, raising a new generation of Oneidas who spoke only English. For some time after their immigration to Wisconsin, the Oneida women still wore traditional calico dresses, but the men dressed in the style of their white counterparts, wearing overalls or pants and button-down shirts. Many nineteenth-century visitors to the reservation at Duck Creek wrote that the community was designed and ordered like any rural white settlement. However, the Oneida continued to be governed by chiefs and tribal councils.

The Oneida population in Wisconsin grew quickly, reaching 1,732 by 1887. As in New York, the community was divided along religious lines. The First Christian and Orchard parties were the two largest groups, and their settlements were surrounded by smaller neighborhoods. The Episcopalian First Christian Party lived at the north end of the reservation, while the much smaller Methodist Orchard Party lived at the south end. The Pagan Party settled in an area called Chicago Corners. Members of different neighborhoods or religions were competitive and rarely married or traded with one another.

However, the neighborhoods did come together to lead the reservation. A governing tribal council was made up of chiefs, known as the "big men," chosen by the Oneida people. One head chief was chosen to lead the others. The chiefs served as lawmakers and judges. They oversaw the use of the nation's communal lands. The Oneida experimented with other forms of government, but continued general tribal meetings in which every Oneida had a vote. In 1925, the Oneida officially reinstituted the old system in which they were represented by nine chiefs and nine sub-chiefs.

This photo shows Oneida girls in a sewing room. It was taken around 1910.

Seven

The Allotment Act of 1887

Wisconsin became a state in 1848, and throughout the 1840s and 1850s, Wisconsin saw a flood of white settlers. They were drawn to the western frontier by the booming lumber industry. Once again, the Oneida were threatened by the approach of white settlements. The success of the Wisconsin lumber business was largely dependent on harvesting white pine. After the southern and central part of the state was nearly cut bare, lumber companies turned toward the reservation and its rich forests.

The U.S. government claimed that it officially owned the reservation land and all its natural resources. The local Indian agent held control over the sale of timber cut by the Oneida and required them to sell it to white-owned lumber mills. Through these agreements, the Oneidas would be paid for their work, but the money paid for the lumber would go to the government.

To gain control over the natural resources available on their lands, some Oneidas supported the division of tribal lands into privately owned plots. Chiefs Daniel Bread and Jacob Cornelius led the party that supported allotment. Cornelius Hill and an Episcopalian missionary named E. A. Goodnough led a group that strongly opposed allotment, arguing that the traditional organization of tribal

The law once permitted companies to remove trees from Oneida lands without paying the Oneida for the lumber. This 1908 photograph of lumber workers was taken in Neopit, Wisconsin, a small town within the Menominee Reservation.

lands maintained the nation's unity and power. The debate raged for almost twenty years and divided the tribe into two groups.

The chairman of the Senate Indian Committee in the late 1880s was a man named Henry Lauren Dawes, a senator from Massachusetts. Dawes and many of his contemporaries believed that the best way to assimilate Native Americans across the country was to encourage them to be independent, land-holding farmers. Dawes supported government-run Native American boarding schools, where students would be taught how to cultivate the land. He also believed that the reservation land, which was owned by the tribe as a whole according to ancient Native American custom, should be divided into parcels for individuals to own. Private ownership of the land, he believed, would create a sense of pride. The Native Americans would no longer

All Native American nations felt the effects of the Allotment Act. More than 90 million acres of tribal land across the United States were lost. The communities that survived were poorly prepared to provide for the growing numbers of unemployed and landless people. Many historians and tribal representatives now argue that Congress's intention was not to assimilate and protect the Native Americans, but to ensure that they would lose their lands. Also, by forcing the Native American off their land, Congress intended to undermine the tribal community and destroy the Native American way of life.

be dependent on the tribal community, which had been the backbone of Native American life for centuries.

The Allotment Act, also known as the Dawes Act for its author, Henry Dawes, became law on February 8, 1887. The law allowed the president of the United States to survey and redistribute the tribal lands of any reservation in the country without the consent of the Native Americans who lived there. Surveys of the Oneida reservation in Wisconsin began in 1889, and the tribal lands were placed in the private ownership of Oneida residents in 1891. Before the land was divided among the residents of the reservation, eighty acres were set aside for a government school, which would serve as a powerful tool for assimilating the next generation of Oneidas. The Dawes Act provided that each Native American family would receive 160 acres of tribal land for farming or 320 acres if

Henry Dawes, author of the Dawes Act passed in 1887, wanted the United States government to divide Native Americans' lands into privately-owned pieces.

the land was more suitable for grazing. Children and young men and women over the age of eighteen also received small sections of land. The allotted land would be held in trust, or protected, for twenty-five years. During this time, the land could not be bought or seized from its owner.

However, in the case of the Oneida reservation at Green Bay, land parcels were significantly smaller than what had been

promised in the Dawes Act. The reservation covered only 65,400 acres, while the population continued to grow, exceeding 1,700 residents in 1889. In addition, members of the Homeless Band, a group of Oneidas who had immigrated to Wisconsin after the 1838 treaty outlined the reservation boundaries, were now considered residents of the reservation and were entitled to a section of land. As a result, the head of each Oneida household was given ninety acres, and

46   These Native American children were photographed in front of a government school on the Lac du Flaubeau reservation in 1906. The government-run schools taught Oneida children to give up their traditional language and beliefs.

children and young adults received smaller parcels. Often the land allotted to a family or individual was made up of several smaller sections of land located some distance away from one another, making the land useless for farming or grazing. The Dawes Act set the stage for the near destruction of the reservation.

In 1906, Congress passed the Burke Act, which was an amendment to the Dawes Act. The law gave the government the right to cancel the arrangement for lands held by people the government considered competent, which meant that they were able to speak English and handle money. The land could be taxed and residents who could not pay their taxes could be thrown off their land, which would be seized by the county government. In addition, the Burke Act declared that all allotments of land that were given to Native Americans who died before the end of the twenty-five-year trust period could be sold without consulting their heirs.

The effect of the Burke Act was that the reservation was quickly broken up and sold. Individual landowners did not have the money to pay their taxes, did not understand taxation, died, faced mortgage foreclosures, or were determined by the government to be incompetent and thus incapable of owning land. As a result, the territory owned by the Oneida Nation was reduced to plots of land that were too small to farm. The lumber business operated by non-Oneidas destroyed the timber resources and the natural habits of the animals that lived there. The economy of the Oneida had to change.

Eight

Oneidas in the Twentieth Century

At the beginning of the twentieth century, the Oneida of Wisconsin faced dramatic changes. Improved roads and the introduction of the automobile encouraged interaction with white communities. White teachers at the reservation's district schools continued to forbid the students to speak in the Oneida language. Grocery stores and gas stations on the reservation were owned and operated by whites. Many young Oneidas went to government boarding schools in Pennsylvania, Virginia, and Kansas. Many did not return to the reservation, choosing instead to take jobs in nearby urban centers, such as Green Bay and Milwaukee, Wisconsin. Government programs continued to encourage Native Americans to explore job opportunities off the reservation, which many Oneida did.

Following the national economic depression of the 1930s, many Oneidas were forced to return to the reservation looking for work, but the Native American community had suffered from the Great Depression as well. The average Oneida family owned only ten acres of land, making large-scale farming impossible. The supply of food was limited, causing the Oneidas, like many other people at the time, to depend heavily on handouts from the government

This photo of an Oneida classroom was taken around 1910.

relief office. Many Oneidas lived in poverty and many were unemployed. They shared small log and wood frame houses, most without electricity and running water.

Despite this economic depression, the Oneida worked to maintain a strong social fabric. Community aid organizations known as Soup Societies collected dues from its members. The money would be used to support the family of a sick or recently deceased member. The Oneida came together to build houses and churches, care for the sick, and entertain one another.

In 1934, Congress passed the Indian Reorganization Act, also known as the Indian New Deal. It provided aid for Native Americans, but also required the Oneida to have a written constitution and a set of laws that replaced their traditional form of government. According to the constitution, which was accepted in 1936 by the Oneida General Tribal Council, the Oneida nation would be

The Oneida learned to make lace in their local churches. Beautifully detailed lace became one of the items that the Oneida sold.

governed by a four-person, elected council chosen by the General Tribal Council, a group made up of all enrolled tribal members over the age of twenty-one. Though the Reorganization Act brought a new form of government to the reservation, it was not able to solve all of the economic problems facing the 3,241 Oneida residents. The Oneida people made a living by planting small gardens, making baskets and lace to sell, and working for white farmers. They also picked cranberries, apples, cherries, cucumbers, potatoes, and beans on local farms. Those who had enough land raised beans, corn, and cucumbers for local canneries.

It was not until the 1970s that the Oneida began to recover from three hundred years of exploitation and loss. Government grants made economic improvements possible. The Oneidas once again pursued their claims to their New York lands. Today, the Oneida believe that the treaties negotiated by independent businessmen and greedy politicians without the consent of Congress following the passage of the 1790 Trade and Non-Intercourse Act are illegal and are not binding contracts. Many other displaced Native American nations have taken up the same fight, and the Supreme Court has heard numerous similar cases. In 1985, the Supreme Court ruled that the Oneida lands were taken illegally. The Court ruled that in all cases, treaties must be interpreted in a way that is most favorable to Native American claims, because this is the way the Native Americans of the past understood them. The Oneidas continue to fight for their New York homeland.

Nine

Oneidas Today

Today, the Oneida Nation in Wisconsin is thriving, with 14,745 members. About 5,450 of the Oneidas live on or near the reservation. The rest of the Oneidas live off the reservation in cities throughout the United States. Because the Dawes Act caused the Oneidas to lose most of their land, the majority of the people who live within the boundaries of the Oneida reservation are non-Native Americans.

The tribal government has a yearly budget of about $262 million, which is used to provide many services for the nation's members: government, health care, education, environmental protection, a history office, planning, recreation, transit, arts, social services, museums, libraries, police officers, veterans' services, and Oneida language classes. The reservation employs more Native Americans and non-Native Americans than almost any other business in the country. It is home to a large industrial park, a printing press, an electronics manufacturing plant, a cattle ranch, an orchard, and a specialized farming community that uses the traditional methods of earth-friendly farming to provide food and trade crops to the Oneida community.

This painting by Oneida artist Lisa A. Fifield is called "Stars in Her Mouth." In it, a woman holds many emblems of Native American history, such as native dress, traditional bead and quillwork, dolls, and weapons.

The passage of the Indian Gaming Regulatory Act in 1988 confirmed that Native American territories are sovereign nations and are allowed to permit gambling on their lands. As a result, the Oneida built the Oneida Bingo and Casino, which provides employment and entertainment to Native Americans and non-Native Americans alike. Sixty percent of the government's budget comes from gambling.

Beginning with the government-sponsored Works Progress Administration's Writers Program in the late 1930s and continuing to this day, the Oneida have made great strides in preserving their language and the traditions of their ancestors. Historians and cultural anthropologists in the Writers Program recorded hundreds of stories and personal accounts as related by Oneida elders. The oral tradition has been written down and translated into English, providing a valuable record of the language and traditions of the Oneida. Today, Oneida historians continue to record the stories that have been passed down through the ancient oral tradition. The nation established the Oneida Tribal School for students from kindergarten to twelfth grade and sponsors programs to teach the Oneida language to children. Historians at the Oneida Nation Museum, the Oneida Library, and the Oneida Cultural Heritage Department preserve, exhibit, and study the historical documents that chronicle the history of the nation. Other residents lead classes in making lacrosse sticks, pottery, and lace, and in weaving and basket making. The traditional prayer of thanksgiving is repeated at the beginning of government meetings, and the festivals of the harvest calendar are once again celebrated on the reservation. The people of the Sovereign Nation of Oneida continue to work to make sure that their community thrives and endures.

Traditional Oneida arts, such as basketry, have continued to thrive over the years.

Timeline

Ancient times/1500	The Iroquois Confederacy is created.
1609	Dutch traders arrive in central New York.
1766	Presbyterian minister Samuel Kirkland settles near Fort Stanwix.
1775–1783	The American Revolution is fought. The Oneida fight on the side of the patriots.
1784–1785	In 1784, the U.S. government signs a treaty promising to protect and maintain Oneida lands forever. New York State negotiates the first of several treaties to purchase land from the Oneida.
1790	Congress passes the Trade and Non-Intercourse Act, making it illegal for states or individuals to negotiate treaties with Native American nations without the permission and presence of a government-appointed Indian agent.
1794	The Treaty of Canadaigua is signed, again promising the Oneida that their lands will be protected by the U.S. government.

1816–1822	Episcopalian missionary Eleazer Williams settles on Oneida lands. In 1821, he negotiates the purchase of land from the Menominee and Winnebago Native American nations of Wisconsin. Members of Williams's First Christian Party move to the new settlement in Wisconsin in 1822.
1825–1830s	The Oneida Orchard and Pagan Parties move to Wisconsin.
1838	The Treaty of 1838 is signed, reducing the Oneida lands in Wisconsin to 100 acres per person, which totals 65,400 acres.
1887	The Allotment Act, also known as the Dawes Act, is passed by Congress, requiring Native American nations to divide and allot all lands for private ownership.
1934	Indian Reorganization Act is passed, providing for a tribal constitution.
1970	The Oneida attempt to reclaim the land that they lost.
1985	The Supreme Court rules that Oneida lands were taken illegally.
1988	The Indian Gaming Regulatory Act is passed, permitting the Oneida to allow gambling on their land.

Glossary

alliance (uh-LY-ents) An agreement made between two or more groups to protect the members of the groups.

allotment (uh-LAHT-muhnt) The division and distribution of lands into individual plots for people or companies to own.

archaeological (ar-kee-uh-LAH-jih-kul) Having to do with studying the way humans lived a long time ago.

assimilate (uh-SIH-muh-layt) To make one people or culture similar to a more popular, dominant culture.

chief (CHEEF) A male leader of a Native American group. The Oneida chiefs are selected by the clan mothers.

clan (KLAN) A group of people that trace their relatives to a common ancestor.

communal (kuh-MYU-nahl) Held in common.

competent (KAHM-puh-tuhnt) Mentally and physically fit to be responsible for certain duties.

constitution (kahn-stuh-TOO-shun) A written document that describes the laws and principles of a group of people.

Continental Congress (kon-ten-EN-tel KAHN-gruhs) The meeting of the first representatives of the United States in which the laws and principles of the new nation were set down.

cultivate (KUHL-tuh-vayt)   To prepare and use land for raising crops.

displacement (dih-SPLAY-smuhnt)   Moving something or someone from one place to another.

False-face (FAHLS-FAYS)   An Iroquois medical practice.

ga-lahs (KAH-lahs)   "Lacrosse," in Oneida.

Great Depression (GRAYT dih-PREH-shun)   A time in the 1930s when banks and businesses lost money, causing many people to lose their jobs.

Indian agent (IN-dee-uhn AY-juhnt)   An official representative of the U.S. government who oversees the government's policies that concern Native Americans.

Iroquois Confederacy (IHR-uh-kwoy)   The nation of Native Americans made up of the Oneida, Onondaga, Seneca, Cayuga, Mohawk, and Tuscarora tribes.

longhouse (LONG-haus)   A long, communal building where several families of the clan live together.

loyalists (LOY-uh-lists)   People who remained loyal to the British monarchy during the American Revolution.

matriarch (MAY-tree-ark)   The female leader of a family, generally the eldest woman.

Methodist (MEH-thuh-dist)   A member of the Methodist church.

mills (MIHLZ)   Machines that process raw, natural materials such as flour and lumber.

missionary (MIH-shuh-ner-ee)   A person who lives with a group of people in order to convert them to a particular religion.

patriots (PAY-tree-uhts)   People who love their country.

portages (POHR-tihj-ez)   A route over land for carrying boats.

preemptively (pree-EHMP-tihv-lee)   Given or sold to someone before others have a chance to bid.

sovereign (SAH-vuh-ruhn)   A nation or people who govern themselves.

speculators (SPEH-kyuh-lay-tuhrs)   People who buy land or trade goods and sell them at higher prices.

surveyor general (suhr-VAY-ur JEH-nuh-rahl)   A government official in charge of surveying, or reviewing, the lands in a state or territory.

swidden (SWIH-den)   Clearing the land by burning the ground cover.

treaty (TREE-tee)   An agreement between two nations.

Resources

BOOKS

Campisi, Jack, and Laurence M. Hauptman, ed. *The Oneida Indian Experience: Two Perspectives.* Syracuse, NY: Syracuse University Press, 1998.

Carlson, Leonard A. *Indians, Bureaucrats, and Land: The Dawes Act and the Decline of Indian Farming.* Westport, CT: Greenwood Press, 1981.

Elm, Demus, and Harvey Antone. *The Oneida Creation Story.* Lincoln, NE: University of Nebraska Press, 2000.

Graymont, Barbara. *The Iroquois.* Broomall, PA: Chelsea House Publishers, 1998.

Kalman, Bobbie, and Lewis Parker. *Life in a Longhouse Village.* New York: Crabtree Publishing, 2001.

Strong, Moses M. *History of the Territories of Wisconsin.* Madison, WI: Democrat Printing Co., State Printers, 1995.

Venables, Robert W. *The Six Nations of New York.* Ithaca, NY: Cornell University Press, 1995.

ORGANIZATION

Oneida Nation Museum

W892 EE Road

P.O. Box 365

Oneida, WI 54155

(920) 869-2768

WEB SITES

Due to the changing nature of Internet links, PowerKids Press has developed an online list of Web sites related to the subject of this book. This site is updated regularly. Please use this link to access the site:

www.powerkidslinks.com/lna/oneida

Index